No, You Can't!

Written by
Rob Waring and **Maurice Jamall**
(with contributions by **Julian Thomlinson**)

Before You Read

to clean (something)

to lie

to race

to ride

accident

arm → and leg →

clothes

corner

dinner

garage

helmet

hospital

motorbike

broken

Anthony

Granddad

Ray

Mom

"I can't wait!" thought Anthony. "It's only four more days."
Anthony was on his bed, reading about motorbikes. There was
a big motorbike race on Saturday. He loved motorbikes very
much. His bedroom had many things about motorbikes.
"The races look great," he said to himself. "I really want to go!"
"I hope Mom says I can go," he thought.

Anthony had homework, but he wasn't studying. He was thinking about being a motorbike racer one day. He wanted to be in a big race. He was winning. He was a great racer. He was strong, fast, and very good. He could hear people calling his name, "Anthony! Anthony! Anthony!"

Then he heard his mother. "Anthony, come here," called his mother. "Dinner's ready." Anthony got off his bed and went down to his mother.

"Are you doing your homework, Anthony?" asked his mother.

Anthony replied slowly, "Umm . . . I finished it, Mom. What's for dinner?" His face was a little red. She looked at him. "I don't believe you. You were thinking about motorbikes again. Show me your homework, Anthony," said his mother.

"I'll show you later, Mom," he said.

"Umm . . . , Mom," he said slowly. "There are some motorbike races this Saturday? Can I . . ."

Before Anthony could finish, his mother replied, "No, you can't!"

"But Mom . . ." said Anthony. "My friend Ray is going. It's going to be great."

"No means no, Anthony," she said. "You know I don't like motorbikes. You know they are dangerous. Please understand."

"But Mom, I only want to *watch* them. I'm not going to ride one," he said. "I can go with Granddad. He likes motorbikes."

"No, you can't!" she said strongly. "And don't ask again."

The next day, Anthony was talking with his friend Ray about the big races on Saturday.

"What time do we meet on Saturday, Anthony?" asked Ray.

"I'm sorry, but I can't go," said Anthony sadly.

Ray said, "What? You can't go? Why?" He was very surprised.

"Don't ask!" he replied. "Ask my Mom! She always says 'No, you can't'."

"That's too bad!" said Ray.

Ray asked, "What are you going to do?"

"I don't know," replied Anthony. "I tried everything. But I have to find a way to go to the races. Do you have any ideas?"

Ray said, "Why don't you ask again? Maybe if you ask a lot, she'll say yes. Or maybe if you help her she'll agree."

"I'll try, but I don't think she'll agree," Anthony replied sadly.

They talked for a long time about motorbikes and the races.

At dinner, Anthony's mother was talking to his father.
"Jeff, tomorrow, would you please clean out the garage?"
"I'm sorry, Sue," he said. "I can't, I have to work tomorrow."
"Mom," said Anthony. "If I clean the garage, can I go to
the motorbike races with Granddad?"
She was surprised. "Well, I guess that's okay," she said.
"Thanks, Mom," he said.

Anthony worked all day in the garage. He cleaned the garage very well. He was very happy because he could go to the races. He worked very hard. He really wanted to go to the motorbike races. His mother was watching him. "Anthony is working very hard," she thought. "He really wants to go to the races. I should let him go."

Then she thought again. "But I'm worried. Maybe he'll like motorbikes more if he sees the races. I don't want him to be interested in motorbikes. They are too dangerous."

Then she remembered her promise to Anthony.

"I promised him. But I want him to be okay. I can't let him go," she thought. "I must tell him he can't go."

Anthony finished cleaning the garage.

"Mom, I did it. I finished," he said. He was happy and smiling.

Anthony's mother spoke to him. "Anthony, thank you for cleaning the garage. But I'm sorry; you can't go to the races."

"What?" said Anthony. "But you promised! You promised I could go." He was angry with his mother.

"Yes. Yes, I know I promised," she said. "I feel bad, but motorbikes are too dangerous for you. And I don't want you to get hurt. That's more important."

"But Mom, you promised!" he said.

"I'm sorry, Anthony. But you're not going," she said.

Anthony went back to his room. He was very angry with his mother.

"It's just not fair!" he thought. "She promised. And now I'll never go and see the races. Ray can go, but I can't. I worked hard in the garage all day. Why can't I go? It's just not fair. Why is my family like this?"

Then he had an idea. He thought, "I can ask Granddad. He may take me."

Anthony decided to tell a lie to his grandfather.

He picked up the phone. He called his grandfather.

"Oh hi, Granddad," he said.

"Hello, Anthony," he said. "How are you?"

"Great!" he lied. "Umm . . . Mom said I can go to the motorbike races on Saturday. Can you take me?"

"Really? Your mom said it was okay? Then sure, I'd love to take you," he said.

Anthony said, "Thanks, Granddad. I'll come over to your house on Saturday."

On Saturday, Anthony said to his mother, "Mom, I'm going out."
"Okay, Anthony," she said. "Where are you going?"
He did not want to tell his mother about his plan. He did not want
her to be angry. "I'm going to Eric's house," he lied. "Then we're
going into town to look at the stores. I'll be back around 6
o'clock."
She replied, "Okay, have a good time."
"Yeah, see you later," he said.

But Anthony did not go to Eric's house. He went to his grandfather's house. He often went to his grandfather's house to look at his motorbikes.

"Hi, Granddad," he said.

"Anthony, it's good to see you!" his grandfather replied. "Are you ready to go the races?"

"Yes," he said. "Can we leave now?"

"We can go later. Come in here. I have some news. I want to show you something," his grandfather said.

Anthony went into the garage. He saw his grandfather's motorbikes.

"Wow, Granddad!" he said. "Cool!" There were many motorbikes there. They were all old, interesting motorbikes.

"I bought this old one last week. Do you like it?" he asked.

"Yes, I do. I love all your old motorbikes, Granddad," said Anthony. He was very excited. "They're so cool."

His grandfather replied, "Yes, they are, Anthony. Do you want to sit on them?"

"Yes, please!" said Anthony.

His grandfather showed his favorite motorbike to Anthony.
"That's one of my favorites," said his grandfather. "I bought
that when I was nineteen."
Anthony was sitting on a very old motorbike. It was really cool.
"These motorbikes are great," he said.
"Be careful with the motorbike, Anthony," said his grandfather.
"What do you think of it?"
Anthony replied, "I really like this one."
"Me, too," said his grandfather. "It's very old."

Anthony's grandfather put on his motorbike clothes.
"Wow!" said Anthony. "You look so cool!"
His grandfather replied, "Put on this helmet, Anthony.
And these clothes."
Anthony said, "Great! Are we going to the motorbike
races, now?"
His grandfather said, "Yes. Which motorbike do you
want to go on?"
"I want to go on that big old one," Anthony replied.

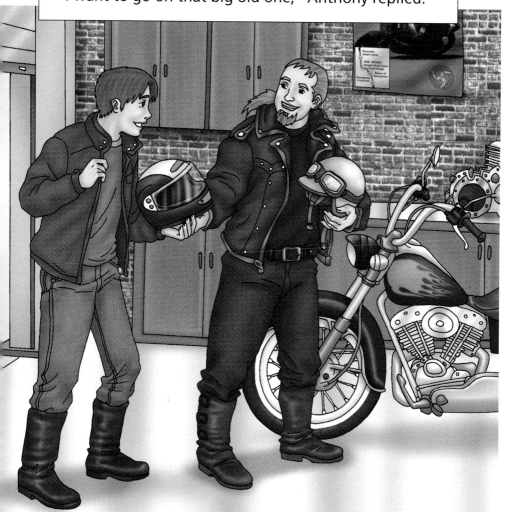

Anthony and his grandfather went to the motorbike races. There were many people and many motorbikes.

"Wow, Granddad. This is great. Thanks for bringing me," said Anthony.

Together they watched the races. The motorbikes jumped very high. They raced around the corners. They went very fast. Anthony pointed at a man riding a motorbike. "Look at that man; he can ride very fast," said Anthony. "I want to be like him one day!"

Anthony saw his friend Ray. He was very surprised to see Anthony at the races. Anthony told him about his grandfather's motorbikes. They talked about the races. They had a good time watching the races.

"This is so cool," said Anthony.

"Yeah, I know," said Ray. "Look at that rider. He's great!" He pointed at a rider.

Then Anthony got a phone call. He answered it.

It was his mother. She thought he was at the store. She did not know he was at the races.

"Anthony, can you help me?" she asked. "I need some things for dinner. Please buy . . ." and then she stopped.

She said, "What's that noise, Anthony? I can hear motorbikes. Are you at the motorbike races?"

"Umm . . . Well . . . I'm here with Granddad," he said slowly.

"Come home now!" she said. "I told you not to go!"

"I'm sorry, Mom. But you promised I could go. Then you broke that promise. It wasn't fair to me. I'll come home after the races. I'm okay here with Granddad. Bye," said Anthony.

Anthony's grandfather asked, "Who was that on the phone?"
Anthony knew he was in trouble. He thought, "If I tell him my
mother said no, he'll take me home. I want to see the races, and
I'm having fun now." He decided to tell another lie.
"It was my mother," Anthony replied. "She asked if I was okay.
She said hello to you."
"Oh, I see," said his grandfather. "Is it okay for you to be here
with me?"
"Sure, Granddad," Anthony lied again.

Later they saw Anthony's grandfather's friend. "That's my friend Mick Arnold. Do you want to meet him?" asked Anthony's grandfather. He pointed at the man on a motorbike.

Anthony was excited. "Granddad, do you know him?"

"Come with me," he said. "You can meet him." He took Anthony to meet Mick.

"Bill! Great to see you," said Mick.

"You won again this year. Great job, Mick," said Anthony's grandfather. "This is Anthony."

"Hello, Mr. Arnold," said Anthony excitedly.

"Hi, Anthony," said Mick. "Please call me Mick, okay?"

Anthony's grandfather spoke to Mick. Then Mick said, "Anthony, there are no more races today, so do you want to ride with me?"
"Yes, please!" replied Anthony.
Anthony and Mick had a great time riding on the motorbike. They jumped high on the motorbike. They went round corners very fast.
Ray watched Anthony on Mick's motorbike.
Anthony was so happy. "This is a great day!" he thought.
His grandfather was very happy, too.

"How was it?" asked Anthony's grandfather. "Did you have fun on the bike?"

"Yeah, it was really great," replied Anthony.

Mick asked, "Do you want to ride it?"

"Me, ride the motorbike? By myself?" asked Anthony excitedly. "Yes, please!"

Anthony's grandfather showed Anthony how to ride the motorbike.

"Now, don't go fast," said his grandfather. "Be careful and go slowly. Try to feel the motorbike."

Anthony listened carefully. He wanted to ride the motorbike safely.

Soon Anthony was riding the motorbike very well. He was having a great time. He went round corners but he did not go fast.

"This is easy," thought Anthony. He was not scared.

Anthony's grandfather watched him and said, "You're doing great!"

Anthony was very excited. "This is so much fun!" he thought. "But I must ride safely. I don't want to have an accident."

Anthony rode the motorbike for a long time.

Anthony was having a good time. He was riding the motorbike safely. His grandfather and Mick watched him.

"This is so great!" he thought.

Suddenly, Anthony's mother came. She saw Anthony on the motorbike.

"Oh no! He's on a motorbike," she thought. "I must stop him. He'll have an accident."

"Anthony!" she shouted. She ran to stop Anthony.

She wanted to stop Anthony from riding the motorbike.
She jumped out in front of the motorbike.
"Anthony! Stop!" she shouted. "Motorbikes are too
dangerous for you!"
Anthony saw his mother. He was very surprised. But
Anthony could not stop the motorbike in time. He did not
want to hit his mother. The motorbike hit a tree and
Anthony fell off the motorbike onto some rocks.
"Oh no! What did I do?" she shouted. "Anthony!!!!"

Anthony was in the hospital. He was badly hurt. He had a broken leg, and a broken arm.

"Mom, Granddad. I'm so sorry," said Anthony. "I was wrong to tell a lie. But I really wanted to see the races."

"I'm really sorry, too, Anthony," said his mother. "I was so worried about you. I didn't want you to get hurt. I didn't want you to have an accident."

"Yes, that's right. But your worry made Anthony have the accident," said Anthony's grandfather.

"Yes, I know. I know," she said sadly. "I didn't want you to have an accident like your grandfather did."

"Accident?" Anthony asked. "Granddad, what happened? How did you have the accident?"

Anthony's grandfather told him about the accident. "It happened many years ago when your mother was about 16 years old," he said. "I was riding my motorbike to work and a dog ran in front of the motorbike," he continued. "Your mother thought I died in the accident. That's why she hates motorbikes."

"But Granddad, you still ride motorbikes," said Anthony.

"Yes, I do, but I'm a safe rider," he said. "But your mother never forgot. She said she would never give you a motorbike because she didn't want you to have an accident."

"Anthony," said his mother. "I'm sorry, I was wrong. I love you very much. But my love for you made me worry. And my worry made you have an accident. I'm sorry."

Anthony came home from the hospital. There was a motorbike outside the house.

"Granddad, do you have a new motorbike?" asked Anthony.

"No," he replied. "I don't have a new motorbike. Your mother said I can teach you to ride motorbikes safely when you are better. We'll use this one."

"What? Mom? Is that okay?" he asked. He was very shocked.

"I talked with your grandfather," she said. "He said he will teach you to ride the motorbike safely. He said I don't need to worry."

"Thanks, Mom!" said Anthony. "Thanks, Granddad! You're the best!"